Bumming in Bed-Stuy

- A Memoir

Paul Adler

BHG Books

CONTENTS

1 | ON LIFE — 3

2 | ON TRANSIT — 11

3 | ON WORK — 37

4 | ON CITY LIFE — 43

5 | ON CIGARETTES — 61

notes — 91

notes — 92

notes — 93

Bumming in Bed-Stuy

ON LIFE

1

ON LIFE

October 16, 2017

Every #metoo I see cuts me to the core and makes my heart hurt—but I'm so amazed by the bravery of every woman who has had the courage to come forward and bolster the reality that sexual assault is an epidemic, that reporting it is a painful and often traumatic ordeal, and that we're not doing enough as a society to address it.

ALL MEN, especially the ones who claim to be "woke," need to recognize how pervasive and pernicious rape culture is and that the statistics on sexual assault are valid and absolutely terrifying; I've seen more "me toos" on my timeline today than I could possibly count. No one gives a shit if you have daughters or sisters or a mother or a grandmother. You should be supporting these women because you claim to be a decent person—and the decent thing to do is to recognize that the problem starts with us. It's not just the assaulter, or the rapist, or the lecher. It's the man who sees a woman being catcalled and says nothing. It's the guy who does nothing after friend confides in him that she's been assaulted. It's every man who isn't actively working to end rape culture. It's you, and it's me.

ALL MEN: We can do better. We have to do better. Start by supporting these women who've been courageous enough to say "me too."

May 16, 2017

Is anybody else just, like, really fucking sick of hearing about avocado toast?

I don't care about your bougie spending habits. Our president is leaking classified information to Russia and seeing how far he can tread into despotic territory—while white supremacy is granted growing legitimacy on the national stage and our country remains inactive during a genocide in Syria, widespread famine in the Middle East and Africa, and the attempted dissolution of the world's most powerful (and necessary) political bloc.

The whole goddamn world is ablaze. If you say the phrase "avocado toast" to me, I will smack you.

October 17, 2017

In trying to put my money where my mouth is today, so to speak, I've almost gotten my ass kicked twice by catcallers.

I guess the same dudes who are willing to call a woman "a fat, ugly bitch, anyways" when she doesn't answer them on the street are equally willing to beat the shit out of a small brown guy interpolating:

"Yo, man, that's not fucking cool. That's disgusting and there's a reason that woman just literally sprinted away from you."

This isn't a public attaboy for myself; I'm not trying to pat myself on the back. I'm just saying, all you would-be allies, if you actually mean what you said on social media yesterday about supporting women—about being willing to speak out and interject on their behalf if you see someone being harassed or being put in a dangerous situation—keep your guard up when you do so, because while these misogynistic assholes might not immediately get violent with the women they're harassing, I have an ominous feeling they won't hesitate to do just that if you try to defend those women.

Of course, this is the reality many, many, many women deal with every day—as evinced by yesterday's #metoo campaign—and I do feel markedly foolish pointing out that, while women have to contend with these fucking nutjobs all the time and men often do not, there are people who are willing to hurt you if you don't let them harass women in peace.

But please, by all means, continue to walk the walk. Continue to put your money where your mouth is. Just know there are dangerous, scary, crazy people out there who feel entitled to harass women without interruption, people who will get violent with men who try to prevent harassment or assault from happening. Don't let that stop you from doing the right thing, but don't be surprised if you need to take a punch every once in a while.

January 2, 2018

I just opened the microwave after nuking some sesame chicken for two minutes and found a baby roach under the glass dish. It was still very much alive.

I'm not even going to attempt to discern what kind of dark, awful portent this is, but it bodes most unwell.

January 29, 2018

I got a paper cut from opening a medical bill last night. Now approaching peak irony.

February 6, 2018

Sure, I'm an open book. But I'm the kind you really don't want to read —like 50 Shades of Grey, the seventh installment of the Davinci Code, all the Twilight books, or Eat Pray Love.

February 14, 2018

I don't care if it sounds gross; I'm shortening "Happy Valentines Day" to "HVD."

February 15, 2018

I am not a violent person, but you will absolutely catch these fucking hands if you stand on the left side of the escalator.

September 16, 2018

Apparently, my new conversation starter with total strangers at parties, after a couple strong drinks, is:

"Let me tell you my story of woe!"

Invite me to your parties! I'm a real thrill.

December 26, 2018

I want to start a series of lectures—like TED Talks but, you know, more demoralizing than inspirational.

For example:

"Will We See the Apocalypse in Our Lifetimes?"

"When is it Appropriate to Yell at a Stranger?"

"Our Country is Totally Boned and We Know It."

Comment with fun topic ideas!

April 1, 2019

Someone please talk me out of getting a finger/hand tattoo; I am 30 years old.

April 17, 2019

I don't know who needs to hear this, but if you're behind a locked stall in a men's room and there are other people in the bathroom, please don't go "AHHHH" like you're Samuel L. Jackson in Pulp Fiction and you've just taken a sip of a tasty beverage to wash down a Big Kahuna Burger.

ON TRANSIT

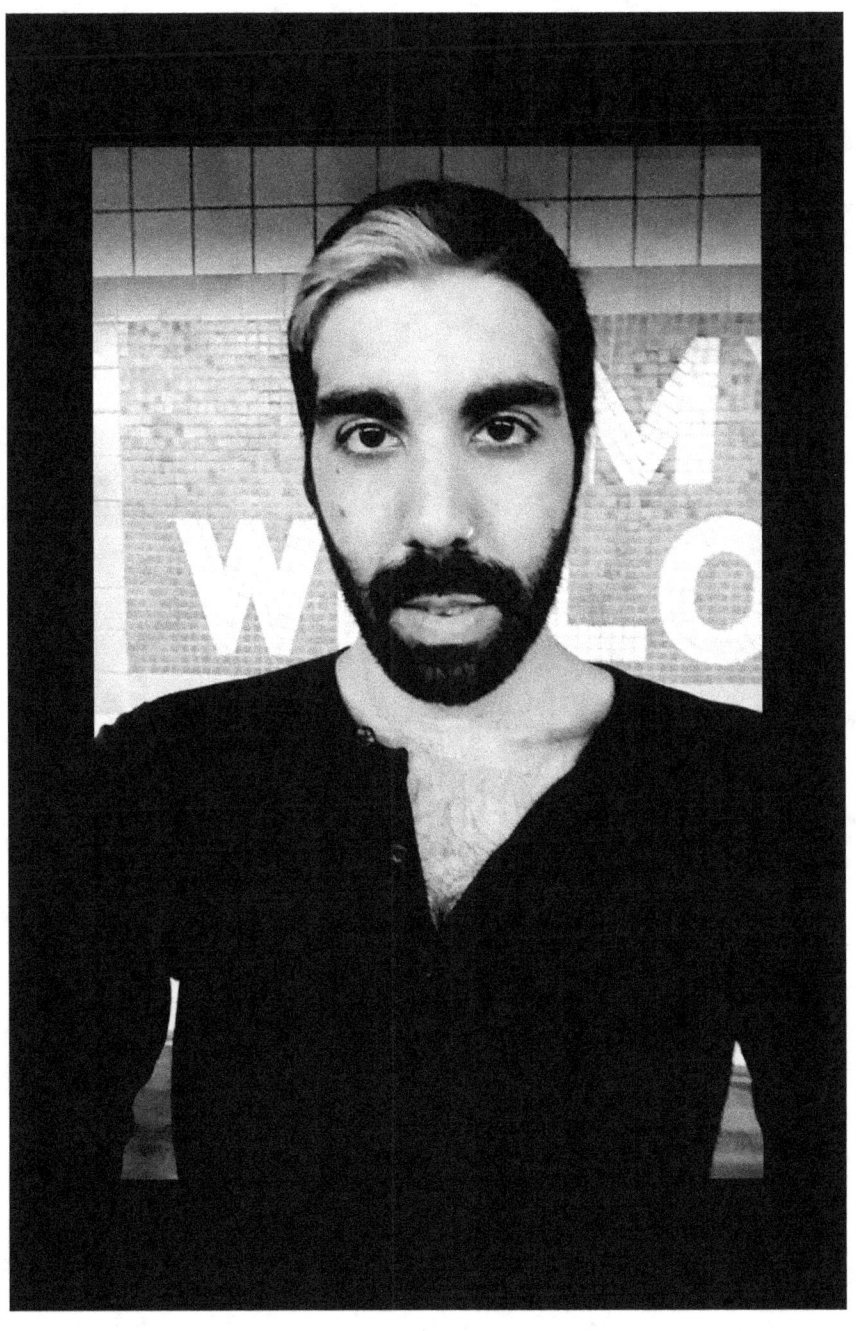

2

ON TRANSIT

April 1, 2016

Back to New York! DC was more than good to me: I saw a bunch of old friends, made some new ones, and drank a ton of delicious craft beer. Of course, my little vacation wasn't without incident or idiocy. I just opened my ticket for the bus and noticed it was for YESTERDAY. The bus driver, unable to scan the QR code in my email, opted not to give a fuck and let me board anyway. Find me at the intersection of blithering stupidity and dumb luck. #blessed #fucked

May 12, 2016

Yesterday, I was on the L train home from work, when I saw a young girl sitting next to me, maybe early 20s, perhaps just back from school. She was brown-bagging it, drinking what had to be a tallboy of Bud Light (so my story probably should've ended there; you get what you deserve for sipping that swill).

Now, I've been given public drinking summons for brown-bagging tallboys of beer before, so I desperately wanted to warn this girl she could potentially get ticketed for consuming that shitty beer on the subway. I also wanted to tell her—a handy, little-known fact about public consumption—that police can only issue a summons if they can identify the make or brand of alcohol; so if you put your wine/beer/ what have you in an empty container without a label, the 5-0 can't do diddly squat.

But then, I realized I would've been giving completely unsolicited advice to a young girl, a stranger, who would probably have found my encyclopedic knowledge of public drinking laws in NYC just a tad perturbing. I'd've been that creep telling you just how to drink your beer in public.

I decided not to say anything.

May 23, 2016

Last night, riding the 4 train to the Upper East Side to watch Game of Thrones and drink fancy wine at Drew Mackasek's place (as is our wont; judge us if you dare), I endured a particularly perilous pilgrimage:

As the 4 train was about to get to my stop, 86th Street, a fight nearly broke out between a big, tough-looking white dude—sporting a du-rag-snapback combo, hand tats, and Beats 'phones—and a smaller, younger, definitely nerdier (I could tell from the Star Wars hat) hispanic kid—maybe my age, maybe younger. I don't know what this kid had done to provoke the white dude's ire, but one second, they were sitting next two each other and the next, they were both on their feet, the white guy calling the hispanic kid all sorts of slurs and begging him to fight. Thing is, though, this big, tough white dude, tryna act all hard? He had with him a pair of Burberry baby shoes. So here I am, watching this wannabe subway tough threaten a kid not much bigger than me, calling him a f****t and a p***y, and I'm thinking, like, "Dude, you're clearly a new father; you really wanna be the guy picking a fight on the subway while holding your infant son's Burberry baby booties in your left hand?"

The rest of the passengers removed their respective headphones as the fight nearly broke out—which, fortunately, it did not—and exchanged knowing looks and muted giggles, like: Look at this idiot, holding his fancy baby shoes and bullying this poor kid over nothing. The rest of the people in the car shared the absurdity of the moment in a sort of beautiful, collective understanding.

And then I got off that godforsaken train.

June 7, 2016

So, here's a fun story—I started yesterday off being harassed by strangers and that's exactly how I finished it.

When my A train got to downtown Brooklyn last night, I tried to transfer to the G back to BedStuy, but it wasn't running, so I had to take a shuttle bus that'd let me off at the stop next to mine. On the way up to the shuttle, I made eye contact with this guy—much bigger than me, with one of those perma-pissed off looks on his wannabe tough guy mug at all times—he asked what the fuck I was looking at, told me I was "looking at [him]," and then followed me up to the street, calling me a f****t and a p***y. He got on the shuttle with me, commenting loudly about what he was going to do to me when I got off, saying he was going to break my face, cut my throat, all that tough guy shit that makes you look like a big man when you're screaming it at a 140lb kid in front of a bus full of strangers at 2am. I couldn't've fought this guy. I've had to fight to defend myself before but one on one, this guy might've killed me.

When we got off at the last stop, the guy started following me home, screaming even more loudly about what he was going to do to me. Luckily, a Good Samaritan, a guy much bigger than the both of us, got in this tough guy's face and told him to back the fuck off. Not satisfied with that, this wannabe bully asked why this guy was trying to protect me—as they were both black and both from the same neighborhood. The Samaritan, whose name I later came to find out was Sean, replied contemptuously that it had nothing to do with race, that he'd been there the whole time, on the shuttle, at the last stop, while this guy threatened me, and while I didn't say a word or so much as acknowledge him. So the tough guy kept at it, telling Sean "you know what he did to me," demanding I tell him I was sorry for some imagined offense, continuing to follow me home, saying that as soon as I turned onto a side street, he was "gonna break [my] fucking face." I haven't a single doubt this guy would've tried to follow through on every single one of his threats once he had me cornered. But Sean, the Good Samaritan, got in between us and held his ground while this goon kept after me.

Lucky for me, we ran into some cops at the next block. Turns out Sean worked for the city and gave them a good description of the guy; they sent out a squad car or two but by that time, this tough motherfucker had turned tail and run off in the opposite direction. Sean and I walked back home together, since we basically live on the same block, and shot the shit the whole time.

At 2am this morning, I saw the best and the worst of New York on a G Train shuttle: belligerent bullies who try to assault strangers for imagined insults, and Good Samaritans who go out of their way and put their bodies on the line to protect people, simply because, as Sean told me, he was sick of seeing wannabe tough guys assault people in his neighborhood for no reason other than to prove how "tough" they are.

Sure, last night freaked me out a bit—I almost had the shit beaten out of me by a total stranger for having the temerity to make eye contact—but it reaffirmed my faith in the people of my city, if only a little bit. I'm glad there are people out there, good people like that guy Sean (whom I ended up begging to let me pay him back with a beer, since he lives half a block away), who won't let violence and threats and intimidation go unanswered, who have the backs of total strangers, just because it's the right thing to do.

June 21, 2016

I'm on the G train in Brooklyn a few minutes ago. It's packed—though I've been lucky enough to grab a seat—but I have to transfer to the Manhattan-bound A. As my train nears the transfer point, I put my book away and stand up. (The nerve, right?) There is no lateral or forward movement; I don't move so much as an inch. But one woman—one steely, heroic Good Samaritan—thinks worse of my intentions.

"Just wait!" she hisses at me, exasperated, as though the mere thought of me pushing past her toward the door has drained her energy to the degree that it takes perceptible effort for her to tell strangers how to behave.

"Excuse me?" I beg, but she refuses to acknowledge my question or so much as make eye contact. She's clearly not having any of it, so I attempt to assuage whatever conflicted emotions she might be feeling and offer: "I wasn't trying to make for the door, but thank you for telling me how to ride the subway—I wasn't sure how!"

Folks, I'm all for correcting gauche behavior on the subway. In fact, you all probably know, at this point, I consider myself somewhat of a paragon of subway civility, of proper comportment aboard public transportation. But I'm pretty sure there's nothing wrong with standing up from your seat as your train nears its destination. I'm not saying it's alright to get up and push past people who are clearly also waiting to disembark upon arrival, but I wasn't exactly doing that—though that didn't stop this courageous would-be subway vigilante from assuming I was. And you know what they about what happens when we assume.

August 15, 2016

Tonight, I experienced one of those rare moments of pure, unadulterated magic between two strangers on the street.

Walking to Penn Station after band practice, I heard, seemingly from out of thin air, the mellifluous tones of Hanson's "Mmmbop" pumping through a set of phantom speakers. I looked around, trying to spot the source of these dulcet sounds, and after much pained searching, I identified the song's origin: this tough-looking, gangster-ass dude—decked out gaudily with a wide-brimmed Yankees cap atop his head, more than a couple heavy silver chains around his neck, and a gargantuan silver timepiece on his wrist that probably weighed more than I do—driving a white Beamer convertible, top down, had that glorious 90s classic absolutely pounding through his car's stereo system.

We made eye contact and for one brief and fleeting moment, we bobbed our heads together, singing that infectious chorus in sync and smiling broadly at each other just before he sped off up Eighth Avenue. Weird, no?

...and now, as I wait for the G train back to BedStuy, I can overhear a girl seated on the bench behind me—a tourist ("I've been in three states in the past 24 hours!")—showing the local guy sitting two seats down from her a picture of a rainbow. A fucking rainbow. And she and her partner are lightheartedly bemoaning the lack of palatable comfort food in the area of Williamsburg where her Airbnb is. And they're laughing together, these strangers.

This is unnatural. It's just not right. Complete strangers don't interact like this, not in New York City.

Shit, maybe it's the heat.

August 16, 2016

What kind of lunatic tries to fight someone on a subway at 9am? Well, let me tell you:

As the G train I was on this morning arrived at its terminus, I got up from my seat, preparing to get off the train, as one is wont to do. Apparently, this was too much for the guy standing next to me, who thought I was trying to push past him and exit the train first (I wasn't; I was standing up so I could, you know, get off the train). Next thing I know, this guy is shoving his way past me, saying something like "Don't try and fucking push past me."

I suppose I made a mistake in responding to him—"Easy, man, we're all getting off the train; I wasn't trying to push past you; I was standing up"—because he escalated, like, really quickly, screaming at me about how I was "talking to the wrong n***a" and how he was going to knock my front teeth out ("YOU LIKE YO TEETH, MAN?! YOU LIKE YO TEETH??").

Sure, I should've ignored this guy from the beginning, but I'm not down with being intimidated by some jacked-up asshole for no good reason at 9am. So I laughed at him a little, along with the people standing around me, who were clearly tickled at witnessing a grown man flip out over an entirely perceived slight. Of course, this made the tough guy even more incensed. He wasn't going to be ignored, and continued to scream about wanting to knock my teeth out.

Eventually, I did make my way past this gentleman to catch my transfer, simultaneously amused at his early-morning insanity and shaken up at the idea of almost getting in a fight for doing something as simple as standing up on the subway.

October 9, 2016

'Bout an hour and a half ago, I'm heading to the L at Bedford Ave and this guy—clearly some sort of heavily intoxicated—walks up to me near the entrance and goes "AYO MAN, WHERE I CAN TAKE A PISS?!" And I'm like, "what? Excuse me?"

"I NEEDA TAKE A FUCKIN PISS WHERE CAN I DO THAT?"

"Uhhhh try Starbucks? It's two blocks up the street—"

"STARBUCKS TOO FUCKIN FAR I GOTTA TAKE A PISS NOW."

This guy is literally screaming at me on the sidewalk as I'm trying to enter the subway because the nearest public bathroom I know of is too far a walk for him at all of two blocks away. And so I turn and begin down the stairs into the subway; I look back at him and he's still screaming, and I say "Jesus fuck—why don't you go piss in the street, then, asshole!?" And all I hear as I descend into the subway is the screaming of barely-intelligible, racial epithet-laden slurs at me.

March 2, 2017

If you want to know what'll elicit a guaranteed "Are you fucking kidding me?!" along with a grand, arms-spread gesture of disbelief from me, be the two bros who decided to hug in the doorway of the G train as the doors slid open just now—casually holding up not only the people trying to get on the train, but those trying to disembark. You wanna get a rise out of me? That'll do nicely.

March 3, 2017

I just got up from a seat on a packed A train to let this blind woman sit down, only to realize she can't actually see the seat. I don't want to verbally point the seat out, nor can I sit back down for fear of looking like a jerk either way.

April 3, 2017

I just walked into a near-empty car on the downtown A train during rush hour. My joy at this public transportation miracle dissipated instantly when I realized everyone else in the car was either covering their noses and mouths or straight-up retching. See that grocery cart filled with garbage bags in the middle of the train? Yeah, that could've been garbage. Maybe. But it smelled, oh, I don't know, more like a cadaver or possibly literal shit. Literal shit. The perfect end to the perfect day.

May 15, 2017

I am on the downtown A train witnessing a trans woman sharing a pint of rotgut vodka with a homeless man and a construction worker. Sometimes, this city is actually magical.

June 6, 2017

Hi it's me, your subway pillow—feel free to, you know, nod off.

June 15, 2017

I'm stuck underground between Brooklyn and Manhattan on the uptown A train. I'm reading my book and I've my headphones in—doing what I can not to be disturbed—when a bag lady (clearly experiencing some sort of schizophrenic episode) sits next to me and starts talking to me, loudly, about (among many, many other things): my phone, texting, computers, credit cards, Roman Catholicism, "blood people," and why she won't eat bread but instead prefers large bags of pistachios. She says she doesn't like when people carry batteries around and wants to kill people who have batteries, "like that serial killer... Timothy McVeigh? No, Ted Bundy."

She says she once hit Donald Trump with a shoe and he sued her for $300, cash. She tries to touch my fresh tattoo and says it means that I sell motorcycles for cash; she won't believe it's Hindi. All the while, I've closed my book and taken my headphones out, responding to her with the occasional grunt, "huh," "hmm," or "yeah," so as not to be rude.

But she's still going. The girl sitting across the aisle from me is giving me a look of pure pity as my seat mate cackles loudly to herself, showing me the giant bag of pistachios she claims keeps her sane. She then tells me if I ever get married, my wife will eat our babies. She's still sitting next to me, still ranting—alternately to me and no one in particular—repeating: "suckin blood, suckin blood, suckin blood..." as I get off the train at Penn Station.

July 6, 2017

So I just casually flipped a woman the bird while entering the subway at Herald Square. I'd walked through the turnstile and, seeing the escalator down to the B/D/F/M was directly to the right of me, walked across the line of turnstiles, giving them a wide berth so as not to collide with anyone entering the station. This woman didn't seem to process that and before she'd even passed through the turnstile, she'd thrown her hands up in a "what the fuck?" sort of gesture. Now, such a gesture is extremely typical of yours truly, and I wholly endorse its usage—but only when merited, and let me tell you, folks, this situation didn't call for it. I didn't cut this woman off, nor was I loitering in front of the turnstile and somehow impeding her entry. So I ignored this woman's frustrated gesticulations and proceeded down the escalator to my train.

But then I saw the woman in question, along with her boyfriend, walking down the ramp next to the escalator I was on; she was pointing me out to her boyfriend, mouthing what could've only been the phrase "fucking asshole." (I'm no lip reader, but I've been referred to by that vulgar epithet enough times to recognize when someone's saying it, even if it's inaudible to me.)

Something had to be done.

I proceeded to give her a big ol' middle finger while grinning like an idiot and laughing as her face reddened and she let fly a slew of curses that'd've made the most seasoned sailor blush. Let it be known I usually try to be very judicious in my use of the bird, but this lady was straight-up asking for it. And that, folks, is what you can and should expect for making a big deal and hurling insults at someone who didn't even impede your right of way.

July 14, 2017

There's a dude standing in the stairwell of the Myrtle-Willoughby G train station just smoking the goddamn fattest-ass, dankest-smelling blunt I've ever seen, seemingly unable to give a single fuck, offering people hits and trying to make sales with each crowd of people departing the subway. Gotta admire that hustle

July 18, 2017

Nothing in my life has more adequately prepared me for the so-called Summer of Hell™ (brought to you the MTA, NJ Transit, and Amtrak) than an adolescence spent learning to hold my own in the pit, dodging spin kicks and crowd surfers. Wanna learn how to deal with hordes of angry commuters packed into impractically small stations and platforms? Hit up a show at your local VFW/community center/dingy college basement.

August 16, 2017

I'm on my way to a gig right now, so I'm just the tiniest hurry. I jogged to the G train clutching my cymbal and stick bags, the straps cutting into my shoulders as I hustled to get to the subway. At the stairs down to the platform, two girls—maybe late teens, early twenties—were taking their sweet time descending, with the one farther down the stairs turning around every few steps to talk to her friend.

Both were taking the stairs at a snail's pace, and I could hear the train pulling up. They were far enough apart; I ran—well, attempted to run—between them. Just as I moved between the two girls, the one farther down the stairs turned again to speak to the other, and so it was that I found myself, for a split second, in the girls' sight line.

"DON'T YOU BE RUNNIN' UP ON ME LIKE THAT," screeched the girl below me, eyes wide with shock and rage, face contorted into an expression of absolute indignation.

"Uh, excuse me?" I offered, pulling my headphones out and slowing down—mistake.

"I SAID DON'T YOU BE FUCKIN' RUNNIN' UP ON ME LIKE THAT. FUCK YOU."

"Oh, sorry, excuse me! I was just trying to get to the train that just pulled up, I'm SO sorry." I didn't have the time or patience to see if the mordant sarcasm in my "apology" registered because I had a train to catch.

In one swift motion, I popped my earbuds back in, pulled out my metrocard, swiped myself through the turnstile, and boarded the train. All I heard from both girls was indecipherable noise as they entered the train behind me, catching it just as the doors closed. For the next half-dozen-or-so stops we shared that subway car, the girls' conversation didn't change in volume or timbre, so I genuinely have no idea whether they responded to my petty little retort. But damnit, I sincerely hope they spent a good amount of time and effort wasting their breath doing exactly that.

August 21, 2017

I just had an uncharacteristically amiable conversation with a stranger on the subway.

This not-so-shabbily dressed guy was walking through the train car, recounting this bullshit story of how he and his three-year-old daughter moved to NYC with his girlfriend a few months ago, but last night, he and his girl got into a fight, and he and his daughter were summarily kicked out of his apartment. "I took her to this babysitter, but the sitter's done at 6 and I need $16 to buy me and my daughter bus tickets to my folks' house in Scranton, PA..."

Eventually, the stranger I ended up talking to—a very 80s-mob-film-looking character; his hair was slicked back, and his suit was freshly pressed, but he had a broken nose—started laughing at the would-be homeless guy. After the homeless man left the car, this 80s-mobster-lookin fella and I had a good laugh:

"Jeez man," he said to me, "that's the biggest whopper I've heard in years! You want drug money, just ask for it! Don't make up some story about your daughter and your ex-girlfriend." And I laughed and heartily agreed.

Hey, when it comes to liars, it takes one to know one—and that dude was full of shit.

November 1, 2017

Had an interview in Jersey City today. Got an offer before I could get back on the PATH train. Excitedly called my mom from Fulton Street to tell her about the offer. Didn't realize, as I was on the phone and waiting for the subway, that I was standing in a puddle of pee. You win some, you lose some.

December 17, 2017

So, I'm on an uptown A train just now, and this guy—had to be in his mid-20s—is running up and down the train car, hissing and spitting at people's feet, scaring this group of school kids who are on the train with their teachers. Several dudes get up to warn this guy off, and the guy starts filming the other passengers. I'm really close to where he's standing at this point; I look up at him and he turns his phone on me. He starts screaming about how nobody'd better touch him or he'll pull the emergency brake and call the cops right now. It occurs to me he may be schizophrenic and suffering some kind of psychotic break.

As he's screaming and threatening to pull the brake, these two dudes walk up to him and get in his face, telling him to chill out and sit down. He doesn't, and one of the dudes punches him in the face. The guy immediately sits down and starts fake-sobbing and screaming. He then abruptly shuts up and moves to get off the train. Turns out 125th Street is the last stop, so everyone gets off the train, and I hear the teachers whose kids this man scared thanking the two guys who "stood up" to him.

I'm sort of glad this guy wasn't given the chance to hurt anybody, but I'm also pretty sure he was very mentally ill and probably could've been talked down without getting punched in the face. Then again, it might be best not to take chances with people freaking out on the subway— you never know how violent someone might turn out to be.

December 29, 2017

There is a Christmas tree lit up in the westbound tunnel between the Christopher Street and Newport PATH train stations.

December 24, 2017

Just saw Santa waiting for the bus on Nostrand Avenue. Merry Christmas.

December 28, 2017

Right now, my definition of "keeping it classy" is resisting the overwhelming temptation to pick this sesame seed out of my teeth with a Metrocard.

January 11, 2018

On the PATH train this morning, I sat down across from an old Asian woman. We made contact and she immediately made the sign of the cross.

Not today, Satan! (Me.)

February 28, 2018

Just got lucky enough to experience the sweet release that is casually yelling "Hey, fuck you, dude!" at some poor drunk bastard who'd pushed past me on the subway steps only to slump down on the stairs and hold up everyone behind him while he busied himself screaming and cursing at passersby.

Yes, that is a run-on sentence. No, I do not care. That's how good it feels to yell at someone deserving while you commute.

10/10 would recommend.

April 5, 2018

So I call an Uber Pool the other day. The Uber gets to my location and I go to meet it. Walking toward the car, I see the back seat is occupied, and there's a girl trying to get in the front seat. I can hear the driver yelling "Paul? Is your name Paul?!" and the girl is ignoring him. Clearly, this person's trying to get in the wrong Uber. About the time I get to the passenger-side door, she realizes her error and, looking decidedly embarrassed, backs away from the car.

I get in and there's loud-ass R&B blasting through the speakers. The driver asks me once, twice, thrice, four times if the music is alright with me. The two girls in the back seat have requested he crank some R&B, which I'm totally fine with.

We start driving, and one of the girls in the back pokes me in the shoulder to ask if I'm okay with the music. I answer, again, in the affirmative.

I face forward and look out the window, trying to space out while the driver navigates north-Brooklyn traffic. But then, it happens: I feel something stroking my left ear. It's a finger. One of the girls in the back seat has taken to petting the side of my head.

"YO, WHAT ARE YOU DOING?!" I yell, incredulous.

"She really likes your hair!" one of the girls answers back, pointing to her friend. I fix both of them with what should be a self-explanatory glare. I don't know whether to laugh or scream.

Both girls apologize. The one who'd been petting me looks confused and frightened. I surmise, based on the loud-as-fuck R&B and the unsolicited petting, one or both of the girls must be rolling. I feel guilty for fucking up their trip and decide to remain silent for the rest of the ride.

April 9, 2018

Tonight's subway ride is brought to you by: a nice pair of khakis abandoned on the platform.

April 20, 2018

Just caught an Uber from downtown Brooklyn back to my apartment after meeting with failure at the DMV—so my day had already been hellishly Kafkaesque. Two blocks away from my apartment, the driver pulled over to let a Hasidic woman in. She got in the back seat and immediately asked the driver to turn off the radio. Then, she asked me to open my door into traffic so I could get out, walk around the car, and sit in the front seat. I looked at her with incredulity: "Wait, what? No. I live two blocks away."

"Alright," she sighed, as she pulled out a religious text and began reading piously.

At that point, yeah, I could've just gotten out and walked the two blocks, but I'd quickly grown invested in making the rest of my short time in the back seat of that Uber as awkward as humanly possible.

My patience was rewarded when the woman's phone went off just as I was about to exit the car. Her ringtone? Some dirty-ass, hood-ass beat, sounding like the intro to a Lil Jon song or some shit. I couldn't help myself; I totally lost it, put my head in my hands, and laughed uncontrollably until we got to my apartment.

July 5, 2018

I am 90% sure the droplet of liquid that just landed in my hair, as I sit here on the G train, originated from the old, fat, bald white man leaning over me and talking to his wife while bracing himself against the railing with both arms out. An old man just dripped sweat on my head. I am screaming inside.

July 16, 2018

Up until this very moment, I've never ridden a bike in Brooklyn—because given my luck, I am 100% sure I will be mowed down by a car the second I mount this cycle. If I end up as roadkill, tell the world my story.

July 23, 2018

I get on the A train uptown, and sit next to this old, white gentleman—must've been late-70s/early-80s.

He points at my tattoo of a woman with sugar skull face paint and asks me what it's about. So here I am, explaining Mexican culture and a Latin idiom (memento mori) to this curious old man on the subway—the guy seemed totally incredulous at the concept of tattoos—when he abruptly changes the subject and starts in with a "You know, back in my day…" sort of thing.

"I don't understand people, these days. Back in my day, nobody used to shave—I mean their pubic hair!

Nowadays, you see people shaving their genitals, that's how they get warts. Yep, warts everywhere!"

He was still espousing the benefits of au natural pubic hair and its accompanying lifestyle as I walked off the train.

July 27, 2018

Things that might be considered "the goddamn devil:"

1. White women
2. The MTA
3. That dive bar where the one toilet has diarrhea in it
4. People who walk too slowly
5. Probably me, if we're being honest

September 6, 2018

New York City: Heat advisory in effect! People are melting as they wait for the subway. The mouth of hell itself has opened up and is ready to swallow Manhattan whole. The end is nigh!

My dumb ass: Ooh, I bet I'd look great in all black today!

September 14, 2018

Most Likely to Get Pushed in Front of the Subway by a Crazed Stranger, 2018

September 26, 2018

The subway, she is a porno / And the pavements, they are a mess / I know you've supported me for a long time / Somehow, I'm not impressed / But New York cares.

January 20, 2019

I've seen a lot of stupid shit in Brooklyn, but watching a teen playing chicken with an oncoming G train, seeing if he could jump back onto the platform before the train hit him, has to be—oh, I don't know—at least in the top three.

October 15, 2018

Now, usually, people get really annoyed when those boarding the subway won't step back to let riders disembark.

And yeah, that pisses the hell out of me—BUT, but—it's almost more incredible to me when disembarking passengers decide to take their sweet time getting off the train: sauntering, not realizing what stop it is till it's too late, and thereby *still* slowing things down by not letting passengers board.

So look, it's pretty simple (unless you are physically disabled or mentally ill; this does not apply to you):

- When the train doors open, you wait till everyone who's trying to exit the subway car gets off.
- When you see someone trying to get off the train very slowly, or not realizing it's their stop and therefore, holding up the train, toss them the fuck out the subway car.
- Ain't nobody got time for this.

January 31, 2019

It's 8am, 4° outside, and being the diligent employee I am, I decide to head into the office early while most of my coworkers are staying home.

I get on the A train and start moving to the middle because it's a bit crowded. There's a guy leaning the entire length of his body up against the pole, so I say, "Excuse me," and go to grab onto the pole.

"What'd you say to me?" he says, taking off his headphones.

"I said 'excuse me;' other people need to use this pole."

"You got a problem?" he says, moving closer.

"What?"

"You got a fucking problem? Cause we can solve it right now."

"Dude, I said 'excuse me.' I just want to hold onto the pole."

He starts to move in and square up. Looks like he's getting ready to take a swing. His wife, seated next to where we're standing, grabs his arm and gives him "the look." Like she's now a Good Samaritan for stopping her husband from throwing hands on the subway because someone said "excuse me

March 12, 2019

Boarding a not-so-crowded 5 train just now, I spy two open seats, for which there are three candidates: me, a young woman, and a middle-aged man. I hang back long enough for the young woman to take a seat, then go for the remaining one. The man, looking somewhat grizzled, just a bit haggard, proceeds to stare absolute daggers at me, muttering something under his breath and giving just the slightest head shake of disapproval, very much in a "fucking kids, these days" sort of manner.

I don't know why that gets to me—I don't usually respond to whiny, entitled behavior on public transportation—but something makes me pull my ass out of that last seat, tap the guy on the shoulder, utter a "Yo," and cock my head in the direction of my former seat. As the dude sits down, clearly pleased with himself at being able to wordlessly shame me into relinquishing my spot, I realize that, no, there's nothing wrong with him: He's not disabled or exhausted or sick or even particularly elderly—he's just an old dick!

Kudos, you old dick. You win.

March 29, 2019

Nobody:

My internal monologue while on the subway: Fucking WALK. C'mon, walk your ass up those stairs; you can do it. The left side of the escalator is for walking—jesus, will you please move? That nice lady is holding the door open for you! Just go! Fuck!!

April 15, 2019

I am currently stuck in a tunnel on an A train that's been rerouted over the F line because of signal problems. There is a young man standing very close to me, SCREAMING about the Illuminati: false flag operations, deep state conspiracies, government-run legal gymnastics, state-sponsored assassinations—some real Alex Jones shit.

I've been trapped on this train for nigh unto half an hour; there's no sign of progress.

It is 9:30 on a Monday morning and I've already lost the will to live through the week.

I tried to tune him out as much as possible. All I know is there's a very obvious connection between the Illuminati, the deep state, and some sort of government-sponsored League of Assassins—and we sheeple are being kept in the dark by the LAME STREAM media.

April 16, 2019

Really wild how much faith everyone around me on the subway must maintain in me not spilling any of this full, open-ass cup of coffee on them.

April 24, 2019

Nothing quite so intimate as feeling a stranger's hot, damp breath on the back of your neck, standing in the middle of a packed subway car, stuck in a tunnel during rush hour. Damn, at least buy me dinner first, my guy.

June 10, 2019

I'm on the L train out to Williamsburg when a girl I matched with on Hinge boards and stands right next to me. Neither of us says a word; we just exchange glances at each other over our phones when we think the other one isn't looking.

This is dating in Brooklyn.

June 21, 2019

Running to catch the G train from my local stop with Ryan Vons just now. We're wearing normal attire (read: all black for me, jeans and a black tee for Ryan), and sprinting down the stairs as the train arrives, when a group of teens goes: "Yo, they look like undercover cops. You undercover cops??"

I shoot a glance back at them—one of unadulterated contempt and indignation—and simply reply, "Hey, fuck yourselves!"

I guess they realized how ridiculous and insulting their question was because they all started laughing somewhat good-naturedly.

I don't know what state of mind you'd have to be in to look at me—me of all people—and think "cop," but I certainly do not envy those dumb teens.

ON WORK

3

ON WORK

July 28, 2016

I'm at my new office, and I go to take the elevator downstairs so I can grab lunch. I get in the elevator and hold the door for this bespectacled, slightly sweaty, middle-aged, bearded gentleman. I push the "Lobby" button; it lights up and the door closes. Before the elevator starts moving, this gentleman proceeds to, while making direct eye contact with me, slowly and deliberately press the "Lobby" button again—as if I hadn't pressed it literally two seconds before. He looks at me, pressing that button with his meaty, clammy forefinger, like he's teaching me a lesson, like he's dying to tell me: "THIS... this is how you press a button, you fucking chump."

We ride down to the lobby in silence—I can feel him staring at me while I keep my eyes trained on the floor. I let him exit the elevator before me.

Can someone explain to me what, exactly, just happened? Because I'm more than a bit confused and I can't quite seem to wrap my head around it. Any thoughts?

April 3, 2017

I'm sitting at my desk at work right now and I get a telemarketing call. Now, I'm not usually one of those people who's a dick to telemarketers—surprise, surprise, right? I mean, they're just doing their jobs.

But for the past three weeks, I've been getting automated calls about a warrantee on my car (disclaimer: In 2012, my car literally exploded while I was driving it). Now, however, there's a real, live woman on the other end of the line. She babbles something unintelligible.

"Excuse me?"

I reply. Something slightly more intelligible involving the word "insurance."

"I'm sorry, what's this about?"

"Sir, your car insurance, sir."

"My car insurance."

"Yes sir, you will need to renew your car insurance, so if I can just get your zip code—"

"I don't own a car anymore. It blew up five years ago. Have a good one."

UPDATE: I just got ANOTHER telemarketing call.

"Hi there! This is Jim. How are you?"

"I'm at work. You?"

"Hahah, well, that's great. Listen, I was hoping to speak with you about the savings you could receive by installing solar panels on your home! Are you the homeowner?"

"No. I'm in my late-20s and rent an apartment; solar power really isn't an option for me."

"Hahahah, okay then! Take care!"

I thought I was signed up for the no-call list. Perhaps, in retrospect, I've been signed up for the no-fly list.

UPDATE: A THIRD telemarketing call. From Florida. About solar panel installation.

"Hello?"

"Hi, this is Greg."

"Okay..."

"I'm calling to tell you about the savings you can receive from installing solar panels on your ho—"

"Look, man. This is the third telemarketing call I've gotten today—and the second one about solar power. No, I don't own a home. I'm in my 20s and rent an apartment in Brooklyn, so solar power really isn't an option for me. Have a good one, Greg."

Jeeeesus fuck. It's never going to end, is it? Am I doomed to an eternity of being polite to telemarketers? This is some Sartrean, "No Exit" kinda shit.

July 19, 2017

In case anybody was wondering: It is 11:20am and I am currently being paid to drink mimosas and eat gourmet donuts.

ON CITY LIFE

4

ON CITY LIFE

March 17, 2016

I didn't realize St. Paddy's Day was an occasion for my next-door neighbors to set off fireworks but, well, here we are

April 13, 2016

It's pretty inappropriate for people to panhandle outside a dollar pizza joint, not because there's anything wrong with panhandling—it's a free country, and it's New York City; you can beg for change anywhere you damn well please—but because of the choice of venue. Like, there's a reason I'm getting lunch at a dollar pizza spot and I can assure you, it ain't the taste.

August 19, 2016

Friday morning in Bed-Stuy.

Trying to get an iced coffee at the bodega around the corner (which normally involves grabbing a solo cup full of ice from the freezer and pouring hot coffee into said cup):

To the cashier: "Hey man, um, you guys are out of iced coffee cups. Think I could get some ice and a cup?"

Cashier: "No. We sold out of them."

"You sold out of cups filled with ice?"

"We sold out of ice."

"You sold out of frozen water...?"

"Yeah, sold out."

Baffled, I walked quite literally next door, to another bodega, to procure my iced coffee. Turned out they had plenty of frozen water.

If you're wondering how something as simple as getting an iced coffee from the corner store can be made into a micro-ordeal, well, that's one way of going about it.

I then found an empty pill bottle (label removed), a foot-long length of insulated wire (tie-off), and a couple dozen hypodermic needle caps right outside my building—which means people are shooting up on my doorstep.

My neighborhood is just oozing charm this morning.

September 19, 2016

Rarely do I have anything overtly positive to say about my fellow New Yorkers—but I think they're to be commended, along with the citizens of my glorious home state of New Jersey, for overwhelmingly keeping their cool in light of this recent spate of half-assed, poorly executed would-be terror attacks.

Many of my friends in Manhattan reacted to the bombing in Chelsea with a sentiment along the lines of "Holy shit, that's awful—wanna head to the bar?" While it's safe to assume most people in New Jersey who've heard of the two attempted, amateurish, unsuccessful bombings in Elizabeth and Seaside Park refused to be intimidated by some lame-ass would-be terrorists, kept calm, and carried the fuck on—as is our way.

We New Yorkers, we New Jerseyans, we've already endured the worst, and we're not going to be scared by some shitty homemade pipe bombs that managed to blow up, let's see, a dumpster and a garbage can. We're stronger than that; we're better than that; and we refuse to let any wannabe "terrorists" break our resolve and damage our spirit.

You wanna try and blow some shit up? Hope the cops find you before we do. Kudos to my New Yorkers, to my New Jerseyans, for standing tall in the face of bush-league attempts to instill fear in us. We're the toughest motherfuckers on the eastern seaboard, and we refuse to be afraid.

December 27, 2016

I'm standing outside my building having a smoke when this guy ambles up to me and sticks his phone in my face, demanding quite rudely that I dial the number on the screen and ask for "Naomi." I ask if his phone isn't working. He says it is but she won't pick up for him. He won't leave me alone and keeps asking over and over until I finally dial the number. It goes straight to voicemail—and he gets mad at me! Like it's my fault this chick's phone is off. He storms off in a huff, back across the street to the Marcy Projects.

And now, I actually find myself wishing he could've just asked me for a cigarette like the rest of the bums around here. What the hell, man?

UPDATE

"Naomi" just called me back and started screaming at me, asking who I am and where her dude "Mark" is. After about 30 seconds of trying to explain what'd happened, why I'd called her, and how absurdly rude her (boy)friend was to me, Naomi apologized profusely on behalf of her man for putting me in such an awkward and bizarre situation. She told me she was very sorry, and wished me a good night.

Now, I can hear someone standing outside my window, screaming "MARK?! MARK! MARK, WHERE THA FUCK YOU AT??!"

The moral of this whole snafu is that I really need to work on this whole saying-no-to-strangers-when-they-ask-me-for-favors-on-the-street sorta thing.

January 3, 2017

"I uhh moved to New York pretty recently, to go to college, so this song's called 'To New York.'"

January 16, 2017

Well, it finally happened—the moment I first foresaw almost exactly five years ago, on that bleak January day I moved to New York City—this afternoon, I got hit by a car.

Late for band practice, I was crossing 8th Ave on 36th Street, right by Penn Station. I had the light, I was in the crosswalk, and that little stick figure of a man was blinking at me, graciously ushering me across the street; I was good to go.

Unfortunately, a driver coming toward me on 36th also had the light and decided at that moment to make a left onto 8th Ave and directly into me. I put my hand out and the car hit me. I mean, it was more of a bump, really. A love tap, if you will. It was barely palpable, though;

didn't even knock me down. But the noise of my open palm hitting the hood of the car—in a futile gesture I somehow assumed would halt the two tons of metal bearing down on me—was enough to draw the attention of everyone on the street. A few dozen tourists gawked at me in that moment, as horrified as they were riveted. I could imagine them running back to their hotel rooms with the news or desperately thumbing a tweet into their phones: "OMG just saw somebody get hit by a car! #NYC."

The driver and his wife, both looking just a couple years shy of 90, stared up at me from behind the dash, dumbfounded. I don't know why I didn't say anything to the grandfatherly old man who'd just grazed me with his car, his thick black shades serving only to accentuate the shit-eating grin spread across his idiot face. But standing there, livid beyond measure, gritting my teeth, arm extended and still resting on the hood of the Honda that seconds prior had almost run me over, I was overcome by something resembling sympathy—along with the realization I was almost half an hour late for band practice. I walked off without a word, sparing everyone involved god-knows-what sort of consequences and resultant legal quagmire pursuant to, you know, getting hit by a car.

April 17, 2017

I am desperately afraid the scowl I keep plastered on my face for things like walking around the city, commuting on the subway, waiting in line, writing and editing copy at work, and basically doing anything in public is going to permanently affix itself to my face, as these activities take up a preponderance of my time. So, if you see me glaring at you, do not be dismayed: I have simply forgotten how to form any other facial expression.

May 16, 2017

Is anybody else just, like, really fucking sick of hearing about avocado toast?

I don't care about your bougie spending habits. Our president is leaking classified information to Russia and seeing how far he can tread into despotic territory—while white supremacy is granted growing legitimacy on the national stage and our country remains inactive during a genocide in Syria, widespread famine in the Middle East and Africa, and the attempted dissolution of the world's most powerful (and necessary) political bloc.

The whole goddamn world is ablaze. If you say the phrase "avocado toast" to me, I will smack you.

June 11, 2017

Just heard what I thought was scratching at my window and, as if out of reflex, muttered, "Better not be those goddamn birds again."

I'd say I'm becoming my grandfather, but he was nowhere near this crotchety.

June 20, 2017

I'm home early, so I thought I'd clean up a bit—you know, take out the trash and stuff. I haul my garbage and recycling down to the curb and drop them. I stand back to light a smoke. Immediately—like, literally immediately—this dude pounces on my trash and recycling bags, unties them, and starts rifling through them. He's taking the beer bottles right now. Like, I understand one man's trash is another man's bottle deposit refund, but damn, no chill.

June 28, 2017

How long do you have to live in a neighborhood before you can start leaning out your window in a wife-beater and yelling at noisy people: "AY. SHUT THE FUCK UP."?

Just wondering; it's summer and Bed-Stuy's starting to get loud.

July 7, 2017

I've just had a terrifying—and, honestly, kind of inspirational—glimpse into my own future:

I'm crossing the street on the way to work, and I'm waiting on the light to change so I can use the crosswalk. The light changes and the "walk" signal illuminates, but a car has run the red light, cutting off the pedestrians trying to cross the street. I stand back to let the car go—so as to, you know, not get myself run over. But one brave old man decides to cross anyway, because he's got the right of way, damnit, and no red-light-running jerk in a Jeep is gonna tell him differently. So this dude, who is at least 70 years old, if not older, proceeds across the crosswalk while screaming at the driver who's cut him off—he's practically leaning into the Jeep's window and screaming: "Fucking asshole!"

This man is my hero, my role model, and definitely representative of my future as a New Yorker.

July 23, 2017

So I just had to walk through Times Square to go to the Guitar Center on 44th, and as I was moving through the crowd, dodging tourists, I managed to knock into someone. I'd just emerged from the bulk of the crowd and hooked a left onto 44th, right in front of the PlayStation Theatre—my destination was in sight. As I turned onto the street, I did a little swerve to avoid one couple, then felt a slight bump as my backpack caught a middle-aged woman by the shoulder. I didn't know it was a big deal until I heard her screaming at me. I took my headphones out so I could better hear her yelling "YOU ALMOST KNOCKED ME DOWN," along with various iterations of "watch where you're going." I started apologizing, just saying very plainly, "I'm sorry; I'm really sorry," but it was no use. People were starting to stare, her husband was clearly over it, I was out of apologies, and she was still screaming. Finally, I threw up my hands, said, "look, lady, it's Times Square," and popped my headphones back in. I don't know what she said after that—all I heard was her continuing to yell.

December 9, 2017

I regret to inform you all today is, indeed, SantaCon 2017. Stay safe, folks; try to avoid the entirety of downtown Manhattan and most of north Brooklyn if at all possible. In the past, participants in this godawful bacchanal have been known to have little compunction when it comes to puking, pissing, and committing very graphic PDA pretty much everywhere you can imagine—and many places you can't.

Beware the vomiting, urinating, sexually deviant Santas coming from all over Long Island and NJ to unleash a wave of filth and publicly objectionable behavior on our fair city. Beware the SantaCon.

January 24, 2018

A short story about my block in Bed-Stuy Within the span of five minutes, tonight:

- This guy tries to sell me an either fake or stolen "diamond ring," claiming he needs money to get his wife commissary (you know, like, the snacks and hygiene supplies prisons sell to inmates). He's clearly on some sort of powerful stimulant. He loses his shit when

I say no, and proceeds to, presumably trying to pull the same con, get kicked out of the bar on one side of my front door, then the diner on the other side.

- Another guy, stumbling drunk, shows up seemingly out of nowhere and tries to barge into the diner next door. When the owner won't let the guy in, the guy starts cursing at the owner in Spanish. The owner slams the door of the diner in the drunkard's face, and the drunk starts pounding on the windows and spitting everywhere. The owner comes back out and he and the drunkard get into a yelling match, the former telling the latter he can't understand him because the latter's screaming in Spanish— the latter screaming at the former some gibberish about how "this is America," etc, etc. When the owner turns around for a split second, the drunk pulls out a liquor bottle and goes to hit him. The would-be assailant, perhaps realizing there are witnesses around, puts the bottle back in his jacket. He backs off a bit but continues yelling. I'm freaked out, so I run to the corner and try to flag down a passing cop car; the cop keeps driving. The drunk guy goes into the liquor store next to the diner and I approach the diner owner. I tell him about the liquor bottle and ask him if he wants me to call the police. He's curt with me and seems more afraid at the prospect of the cops showing up than he does being bottled. He goes back inside the diner and I don't call anyone.

- Simon, a sometime-homeless man who's been living around my block lately, gets out of a cab. He looks like he's been sleeping outside the past couple days; his hands are black. His face is covered in blood. I ask him what happened and tell him to watch out for the drunk guy with the liquor bottle, who's now standing about five feet away from us, leaning up against the wall of the bodega. Simon tells me he just got jumped in the Marcy Projects, which are across the street. I wonder why he just got out of a cab.

As I reach into my pocket and put whatever change I've got in his hand, he tells me he knows I'm high. I'm not. He tells me I'm on a high-grade stimulant—coke, he guesses. I'm not, and now I'm getting pissed off. Last week, Simon was on the corner asking people for money. He'd told me he needed $20 so he could pay a woman in the projects to sleep on her couch. I knew he'd've used the money to buy drugs, so I gave him a few cigarettes, went upstairs to my place, and came back with food for him. The next day, Simon was back In front of the bodega asking for money. I'm furious Simon's just taken my money and played on my concern and sympathy. But before I can say anything more, another guy, "Bill," interrupts us.

- Bill—that's not his name but it's the one he gives me—has four years clean and sober, and has been really nice to me over the past few weeks when I've seen him on the sidewalk in front of my apartment. Bill not-so-subtly lets me know he thinks I've just bought drugs from Simon, who's already in the bodega using whatever money he has, including the change I've just given him, to buy a soda. I'm incredulous: "Are you kidding me? Didn't you just see me give him, like, 50 cents?" "Yeah but you were talkin' to him for too long; thought you were 'indulging,'" Bill says. Agitated, I try to tell him I was just worried about Simon—who, despite being a manipulative, prevaricating addict, does look like he's really just been jumped. Bill seems not to believe me. The B54 bus pulls up and he gets on, followed by the drunk guy who'd just tried to bottle the diner owner moments before. I'm confounded; my head hurts. I finish my cigarette and go back inside, where my girlfriend tells me I'm way too involved with the people on my block.

And she's right.

January 31, 2018

I go downstairs to the deli on the first floor of my office building, to get a bagel. Order a pumpernickel bagel with lox spread, toasted. Head over to the coffee-prep area to pour myself a cup.

Get back and see the two guys behind the counter having a heated argument in Spanish—about the lox spread. One of the guys seems to be explaining to the other what lox spread is, and that it is indeed a menu option, while slicing off some judiciously sized pieces of smoked salmon. The guy doing the explaining then takes, in his gloved hand, a literal handful of cream cheese, mashes the smoked salmon into it, and proceeds to roll it into a ball of sorts, making sure the smoked salmon mixes well with the cream cheese. This Play-Doh-like miasma of fish and dairy is then plopped unceremoniously on a freshly toasted pumpernickel bagel, which is then wrapped and handed to me.

I look at the two guys behind the counter, expecting someone to offer a reason—we didn't have any lox spread so we decided to MacGyver you some, my dude—anything in the way of an explanation for what's just transpired in front of me. There is only silence.

I'm at a loss. I know something viscerally wrong has just happened to me, to my bagel. I cannot articulate it, let alone in Spanish. I accept and pay for my violated bagel, and make for the elevators, head hung low, to go back to my desk and there, eat my shameful meal.

February 5, 2018

Bought premade sushi from the deli downstairs—at 4pm. Really taking my life into my own hands, here.

July 9, 2018

I just witnessed a grown-ass man in a suit slide down a handrail, Bart Simpson-style, at the World Trade Center. Mondays, amirite?

July 13, 2018

Hour five at the DMV in midtown. I've lost all hope and come to terms with the fact that I live here now. Send help, snacks, or substances.

December 8, 2018

Your annual reminder: Today is Santacon. Watch your shit. Don't venture into Manhattan if you don't have to. Beware the ubiquitous puddles of vomit and urine. Watch out for drunk Santas fighting, looting, and possibly fornicating in public.

Remember when the Eagles won the Super Bowl earlier this year and the nation watched in horror/amusement as Philadelphians, with little compunction, staged a full-scale riot and trashed the shit out of their city? Yeah, Santacon yearly makes that bacchanal look like a goddamn 1960s sit-in.

If anybody should like to join me, I'll be watching the drunken bridge-and-tunnel rabble do their worst from a comfortable perch in the West Village, chain-smoking and muttering all manner of cryptic one-liners. You've all been warned.

January 28, 2019

Good morning from scenic Bedford-Stuyvesant, Brooklyn, where it's snowing, there's no heat or hot water in my building, and I am slowly freezing to death inside my apartment. Tune in later to find me deciding which one of my neighbors is edible, Donner Party-style.

Update: Also, the G train broke down this morning and isn't running from my stop. Happy Friday!

March 13, 2019

I'm hungover at the bodega (never you mind why I'm hungover on a Wednesday morning) and this guy really just tried to get into it with me over how long it was taking to pour my coffee.

I've just poured the cup and am reaching for a stirrer when, from behind me, I hear: "Yo, my man, can I make myself some tea or are you gonna take all day?"

"I'm sorry?" I offer. "I'm just finishing up."

"Yeah well I'm waiting, here; hurry up, man"

"Um, I'm just grabbing a stirrer. Can you hold on a second?"

"Your 'second' is taking a minute, man."

And. I. Am. Done. "Are you fucking kidding me?" I manage, my right eye twitching ever so slightly.

At this point, the dude pulls the "YO, THIS IS BROOKLYN; YOU GOTTA MOVE FASTER" card, to which, admittedly, I react poorly.

"Dude, I know. I live next door. Fucking chill out."

"Oh yeah?" he says. "How long, though?"

I respond by flipping him off and exiting the shop, coffee in hand.

Lest anyone think I was the cause of an actual holdup, let it be known that this dude could've literally stepped two feet to the side to grab his cup of tea. Without the argument, I'd've been in and out of the bodega in 30 seconds. I was not in his way, not even remotely, yet he opted to hassle me over a nonexistent slight.

I am being tested. The lord is testing me.

May 25, 2019

So I'm in line at the bodega last night, having just smoked a big ol' spliff and wanting nothing more than a pint of ice cream on which to gorge. The line is absurdly long for a Friday night, but I grab my carton of Mint Chocolate Chip and queue up. I'm not even on line for five seconds when this visibly drunk (like, swaying, slurring, all sorts of tipsy) dude clutching two 24oz bottles of Corona ambles up to me, points at the pint of Häagen-Dazs in my hand and goes, "That all you got?"

"I'm sorry?"

"THAT ALL YOU GOT??"

"Um, yeah. That's it."

"AY," he turns and yells at the cashier, "I GOT THIS GUY'S ICE CREAM."

He turns to me and goes: "You can head out, man. Have a good night."

I thank him profusely and make for the door, pint of ice cream in hand.

I think I'd been blessed by some sort of stoner miracle.

ON CIGARETTES

5

ON CIGARETTES

February 25, 2016

Just had my daily "Curb Your Enthusiasm" moment a few minutes ago: I got lambasted by a mentally ill, homeless woman outside a grocery store.

I'd been sent out by my boss to get coffee creamer for the office. On my way out of the store, I was stopped by a homeless woman who said "Can I ask you a question? Could you spare any money?" I responded: "No, I'm sorry but I don't have anything to spare." (I didn't; the money was my boss'.) As I was walking away, I pulled out my pack of cigarettes to have one and thought to myself, maybe that woman would like a cigarette—cigarettes usually make things a little better.

So I ran back to her and held out my pack, saying "I don't have any money to give, but would you like a cigarette?" She started screaming at me: "I DIDN'T ASK FOR A CIGARETTE. I ASKED YOU FOR MONEY. I DON'T SMOKE. I'M HUNGRY AND I DON'T SMOKE AND I DIDN'T ASK YOU FOR A CIGARETTE AND I DON'T SMOKE..." and she went on like this for a good 30 seconds until I retorted: "OKAY. COOL. SORRY. HAVE A GOOD ONE. FUCK."

Now, in this woman's defense, she did ask for money and not for a cigarette. The situation was probably analogous to someone asking me to write a paper for them on a subject I don't understand and me saying "Oh, well, I can't write about quantum physics, but I can write you a flawless paper on William Faulkner." If someone asks you for money, I guess you should give them what they ask for or nothing at all—and it's not your place to decide what they spend it on. There's a fair amount of literature on this notion.

But in my naïveté and earnestness, I just thought a cigarette might help, and I thought wrong.

June 6, 2016

Monday morning, 10am, the Village, Manhattan:

As I come up the stairs at the West 4th Street station, I light a cigarette. Crossing the street on the way into the office, I'm accosted by two women—not particularly put-together, but certainly not disheveled or appearing as though they might be homeless—the first of whom, with the zeal of an addict looking for a fix, asks to buy a cigarette from me. Now, I've got three cigs left in my pack, and I'm desperately trying to quit smoking, so I'd intended this to be my last pack. When I say, "I'm sorry, I can't sell you one," she replies, "Yeah–yes you can."

I repeat myself: "No, look, I've only got three left; I really can't sell you one." At this point, she and her friend are actively blocking my way, preventing me from walking to work. The first woman asks again and again for a cigarette, and I say "Look, I'm really sorry; I just can't sell you one."

She gets out of my way and screams "YOU'RE NOT SORRY, YOU FUCKING ASSHOLE." So I'm, like, wow, alright, um I'm going to be on my way now, and start walking—her friend screams after me:

"I HOPE YOU GET CANCER IN YOUR FUCKING ASS AND YOUR INTESTINES FALL OUT." Not one to let that slide, I throw a "Hey! Fuck yourselves!" over my shoulder, and flip these dames not one bird, but two, continuing on my way as they shout all manner of obscenities after me.

Happy Monday, New York City.

June 10, 2016

People in this city must think I'm a goddamn cigarette dispensary or something.

I'm smoking a cig outside my office and this young woman, dressed in a very fashionable (read: expensive) outfit, comes up to me and coyly—giving her best, pursed-lips, somewhat-giggly, damsel-in-distress performance—goes: "excuse me, do you have an extra cigarette?"

I respond: "yeah, you got a dollar?"

She coos: "teeheehee, I don't have any cash on me!" flashing her phone case and shuffling through her credit cards to display her lack of hard funds. She clearly still expected me to give her a cig but after about 10 seconds of delivering nothing but a quizzical look, she loped off down the street, no doubt off to find the next sucker who'd be willing to bum her a cig, gratis.

I don't know if I look generous or stupid—but you want a cigarette? You can give me a dollar. You want to act spoiled and entitled? No cig for you.

August 7, 2016

People must think I'm a goddamn bodega or something, because not a day goes by where someone doesn't try buying a cigarette off me. Now, packs are expensive, and the tacitly, socially agreed-upon rate for buying a 'loosie' from a stranger on the street is typically a dollar, as opposed to the $.50 you might pay at an actual corner store.

So this guy comes up to me as I'm about to head up to my rehearsal space:

"Hey man, sell me a cigarette? I'll give you a dollar."

"Well, uh, okay..."

"You know, it'd be really cool of you if you sold me *two* cigarettes for a dollar, but that's up to you."

[À la Bill Lumberg from Office Space] "Yeah, so I'm gonna sell you one cigarette..."

August 29, 2016

A drunk/high transwoman just approached me outside Grand Central and asked to buy a cigarette from me. I named my price, asking her if she had a dollar. She only had $.75, but she looked a mess, so I pulled deep from my near-dry well of sympathy for strangers on the street who try to buy cigs from me and told her I'd accept her $.75. She asked if I had Newports. I didn't. But in telling her I didn't, I well—I apologized. I apologized for not having a menthol cigarette to sell this woman.

To reiterate: I just told a stranger on the street, for whom I'd already made an exception in price, that I was sorry I didn't have her cigarette of choice.

Who the fuck do I think I am—some warmhearted schmuck, a sucker for distress who apologizes for not carrying around menthol cigarettes to sell below market value?

I'm having a mini-identity crisis, folks.

UPDATE

As I transferred to the G train to get back to BedStuy a few minutes ago, I was able to find a seat between a man and a woman. The woman was sitting demurely, legs close together, listening to music. The man? Oh, you'd better believe he was manspreading like he was the only person on the train. For reasons of not wanting my legs pushed so far together they'd create a testicle sandwich—as well as, you know, wanting to stand my ground against blatant discourtesy—I pushed my legs apart. I pushed them to the borders of the seat, just a bit narrower than shoulder-length apart, where they would sit naturally without infringing upon anyone else's space. I pushed back against the manspreader so I could have my fair share of space.

He noticed immediately, and I could feel my right leg straining to hold its ground as this much-larger gentleman (if you could call him that) pushed and pushed against me, hoping futilely to gain back his manspreading space. This went on for maybe three or four stops. Eventually, the woman to my left got up, leaving an extra space. I didn't move. I waited until the dude was uncomfortable enough at the sensation of my leg pressed fast against his, and then he took his headphones off and asked me: "Man, you sure you don't wanna move over?"

"Alright," I said, "but you know, your legs are spread wide as fuck. You see how when I move over, they take up half the seat next to you? That's a courtesy thing. I see you're a reasonable kinda guy, so I hope you understand that."

He put his headphones back on.

Identity crisis: averted.

September 8, 2016

Here's a short and sweet cigarette-bumming tale for you folks:

I'm standing outside my job having a smoke a few minutes ago when this dude staggers up to me and asks if I have a cigarette I can bum him. Per usual, I say "Sure, man, do you have a dollar?"

Homie responds: "If I had a dollar, I wouldn't be asking you for a cigarette."

Okay, dick. Clearly, this gentleman wants a free cig, which I'm not prepared to offer. So I just kind of shrug at the guy. He responds by calling me some type of slur under his breath and stalking away.

Sorry, guy—you want to bum a cig from a total stranger on the street? You'd better have a dollar.

September 23, 2016

Alright, here we go: I just walk down to the bodega around the corner from my place to buy one nice beer for myself and one tall boy of Coors Original for my girlfriend. I light up a cigarette on my way back, intending to smoke it outside my building before I head back inside for dinner.

This guy stumbles up from behind me, clearly drunk as shit, and mumbles "Yo man, lemme get a cigarette?"

"Sorry, man; I only have, like, two left."

"What the fuck, man, I'm just asking you for a cigarette."

"Yeah. Like I said, I'm sorry but I only have two left. You know, the bodega sells loosies for $.50."

"I don't have fucking $.50, man, just gimme a cigarette. I ain't gonna do anything to you." (Implying I must be afraid of him assaulting me because I don't want to give him one of my last cigarettes.)

"Dude. I only have a couple left. No."

As he walks away, he starts cursing me out under his breath, to which I respond, now audibly irritated: "Um, excuse me?"

"I said GOD BLESS YOU."

He turns around, starts walking away, and falls into the side of a building.

"Yeah, man... have a good one."

Seems I can't make it 50 feet from my front door to the bodega and back without some sort of incident hinging around a stranger demanding a cigarette from me. I am a magnet for indigent, drunk strangers who think they're entitled to my smokes. This is my life; this is the story I'm fated to live again and again, like some hellish Groundhogs Day-esque scenario.

September 27, 2016

And now, for the latest in cigarette-related news:

This homeless woman who essentially lives at the bus stop outside my office always seems angry at me. Since my first day here—since the very first time I went outside for a smoke—she's had this habit of staring daggers at me and muttering curses at me under her breath, seemingly for the crime of, well, existing; possibly standing in or near what she's deemed as her space; possibly smoking without offering her a free cig. Naturally, I'm disinclined to bum her cigarettes when she asks, which only makes her angrier and more prone to giving me the "evil eye" while cursing at me.

She just sauntered up to me, holding two cigarettes, and asked me for a light. I took out my Zippo and lit her cigarette for her. She didn't thank me and instead, walked away, looking back at me every few steps to shoot her caustic glare my way, mumbling insults all the while.

I just want to ask her: Lady, why you so mad?

September 28, 2016

Last night, I was standing outside the door to my building, smoking a cigarette, when I was approached by a young woman holding multiple boxes of pizza. This woman, who turned out to be my neighbor, offered me one of the boxes of pizza, claiming she'd just come home from a work event with more leftover 'za than she was prepared to deal with.

"I just gave away, like, seven other boxes," she said. "I promise, it's not, like poisoned pizza or anything," she said. Thinking this some sort of karmic New York miracle, kind of like the opposite of someone trying to bum a cigarette off me, I took a box of pizza from this person. When I saw her open up her mailbox and, shortly thereafter, enter her apartment—but not before giving away another box of pizza to another trusting neighbor—I realized she was telling the truth about living next door to me.

And I believed all her other beautiful lies.

I let myself have a moment of unchecked optimism, which, in this city, can be acutely dangerous. Because that pizza—that goddamn fucking street pizza—did not go quietly. In what could only have been a mild case of food poisoning, it had its way with me this morning, and this afternoon, and again just a few moments ago.

But this wouldn't be one of my tales if things just, you know, got better herein, now, would it?

Because right now, I would really, truly like to know which of my roommates left his dirty underwear hanging on the doorknob inside my bathroom, as there are few surprises less pleasant than discovering you've got to handle some dude's stank-ass unmentionables seconds after pulling up your own in order to get out of the bathroom after going a third round with some bad New York street pizza. And, yes, I'm writing from inside the bathroom—as I'm desperately putting off touching in any manner my roommate's used drawers.

This is hell. This is my hell.

October 21, 2016

My friend just asked me: "Do people ask you for cigarettes like every day?"

The walk between my front door and the subway is maybe—MAYBE—100 feet. Some mornings, I like to have a cigarette while waiting above ground for the train, because I can hear it pulling up, toss my cig, and run down in time to catch it. Today was one of those mornings.

So, I'm standing by the entrance to the G train, smoking a cigarette (not on or overly close to the stairs, mind you; I'm no monster), and this guy, looking a little down-at-the-heels but most definitely not homeless, walks up to me and asks if I can "let [him] get a cigarette." Now, I had my headphones in; I pretty obviously did not want to be disturbed, but this guy really wanted a smoke.

He asks, and I respond: "Do you have a dollar?"

"What?"

"Do you have a dollar?"

"Huh? You *really* gon' charge me a dollar for a cigarette?"

I raise my eyebrows and give a slight nod in affirmation. It occurs to me that this guy, incredulous at my demand of a dollar for a cigarette, is standing a block, block and a half, away from at least four bodegas that sell loosies for $.50 apiece. But this gentleman expects one for free from me, and he acts as if I've caused him some terrible affront when I name my price.

He gets out of my face and starts walking away, but not before screaming—hollering at me loudly enough to turn the heads of half a dozen commuters headed down into the subway—"Oh, THANK YOU. THANK. YOU. THANKS A LOT." He continues with such utterances as he shuffles down the block.

This was my first encounter of the day with a person other than my girlfriend.

So, do people ask me for cigarettes, like, every day? I wish I could say no.

October 25, 2016

Here's a new one: About an hour ago, I'm having a cigarette outside my apartment when this guy comes up to me and asks, in Spanish, if he could come inside for some food. He looked entirely sober and, for all intents and purposes, relatively well off—that is, well-fed, -clothed, and cleaned up. He just kept asking, assuming (correctly) that I understood his Spanish, if he could come inside for something to eat. And, I mean, I had dinner tonight but my pantry isn't exactly stocked to the point of surplus. So I had to tell him, in Spanish, I couldn't feed him. But the whole situation left me wondering if he couldn't've just bothered me for a cigarette like everyone else in BedStuy.

October 25, 2016

Incredible. I don't know what made me think I could have a cigarette in peace before I go to bed.

I just stepped outside, and the second I stepped out, this woman came up to me and started talking:

"You can't smoke in the house?"

"What?"

"You can't smoke inside? I'm just askin'." She gestures across the street. "I'm from the projects."

"What? Uhh... no. I can't smoke inside."

"Oh, can you spare a cigarette?"

"I left my pack inside."

"Oh. You could maybe spare a dollar, then?"

I'm wearing pajamas. All I have on me is my phone, keys, lighter, and the one cigarette I just lit. I explain this to her. She's genuinely put off at my immediate lack of cash, but stops just short of asking me to go back inside when I tell her I don't have any cash in the apartment, either. I don't know why I had to explain myself in such depth but then again,

I don't know why I can't just walk outside for a goddamn cigarette without issue.

October 28, 2016

I swear, there is no way this shit isn't actively haunting me.

In the two stops between where the 7 train embarks at Hudson Yards-34th Street, and where I got on at Grand Central, two guys got in a fight, which I walked into the middle of as I was trying to board. I mean, I say "fight," but really, it was this big, bald, drunk asshole with really severe plumber's crack trying to assault some little wiener dude —who sounded remarkably like Steve Buscemi as he was screaming: "Help! He's assaulting me! Somebody call the cops!"

Naturally, as all horrible New Yorkers do, the bald asshole tried to invoke our fair city in screaming something unintelligible back at the guy. Though I couldn't quite make it out, it sounded something like: "Eyyyy. Take a picture 'a ME, will ya!?! This. This is New. YAWK. CIT-TAAYYY." He continued in this fashion until somebody forced him off the train.

Whatever specter of violence, menacing, and wanton cigarette bumming is haunting me, I think you done pissed it off with your artwork.

November 8, 2016

Odd morning for cigarette requests:

I was just outside smoking, and I saw this homeless man shuffling down the street toward me, sobbing—he looked absolutely distraught. He asked a woman standing about ten feet away from me for a cigarette; she didn't have one. Had he asked me, I'd've actually given him a smoke.

He did not ask, and instead, kept on moving down the sidewalk, tears streaming down his face.

About a minute later, a man in a suit approached me: "Hey, man, is there any chance you have an extra cigarette?"

"You got a dollar?"

The man took out his wallet and opened it up; he didn't have any cash on him. Instead, he took out a broken debit card and told me he was on his way to the bank to get it replaced, then said "thank you" and walked away. I absolutely didn't need to know—nor did I care—about his debit card situation or the fact he was headed to the bank. But I did appreciate his politeness at being refused a cigarette for lack of hard cash.

I'd still rather have given a cigarette to that homeless man, had he approached me and asked.

November 22, 2016

Starting early today:

I'm outside my office finishing up a smoke when this guy walks past me, looking a bit disheveled but not particularly indigent, let alone homeless.

He starts in: "Can I get a cigarette?"

"Sure, you got a buck?"

"A BUCK?! SCREW YOU."

"Uh, excuse me?"

"I SAID SCREW YOU."

"Uhh, okay, then: fuck yourself?"

"DIDN'T YOU HEAR ME? I SAID SCREW YOU!"

"Yeah, no, I got that. Go. Fuck. Yourself. Later, dude."

And with a flip of the bird, he was on his way.

I mean, jeez, how dare I have the temerity to ask for money in exchange for a cigarette? Great way to start a Tuesday morning.

November 30, 2016

I've just encountered a new and special kind of discourtesy in the realm of the Public Cigarette Exchange:

I'm outside my office having a smoke when a woman walks up to me, an unlit cigarette in her hand. She's on the phone and gestures with a slight nod at her cigarette.

She does not use words; she's far too occupied by her phone conversation to verbalize her want of a light. There's no "please" or "thank you," just a look of vicious contempt when I take more than five seconds to realize her looking back and forth from my cigarette to hers means she wants a light.

Oh, and she can't light her own cigarette—how could she? She's got her phone in one hand and her unlit smoke in the other; her phone call takes priority over the real-life interaction taking place. God forbid she tell the person on the other end of the line to hold on for a damn second so she can do things like: use her words to ask for a lighter, take the lighter from my hand, and use my lighter to light her own cigarette. No way, nuh uh—she's far too important to be bothered by such trivial, silly notions as common courtesy or, you know, decency.

She continues looking at me, visibly annoyed I haven't yet lit her cigarette for her. I light her cigarette for her. (She works in my building; I don't want to make an enemy by asserting my ridiculous expectation of courtesy.) There is no "thank you;" there's no acknowledgement of any kind; and if you think there's so much as a smile—well, you, dear reader, are quite mistaken. I'm a human cigarette lighter; I exist solely to ignite this woman's Marlboro Red.

Her cigarette lit, she promptly turns on her heels and walks away in a huff, continuing her phone call. She seems even more annoyed it took a rube like me so long to acquiesce to her silent demand for a lit cig. She stops a few feet away and turns her back to me.

The woman finishes her smoke before I finish mine, and hangs up her phone. She marches past me and into the building without exhibiting even the slightest awareness of my existence, let alone the service I'd just provided her.

As I'm finishing my smoke and writing this status, a man walks up to me: "Can I puh-leeeeaze bum a cigarette? Please?!"

"Man, I left my pack inside. I'm sorry." (This is the truth.)

"Ah, shit, that's alright—you have a good day!"

[Five seconds later, to another man smoking outside the office]: "Can I puh-leeeeaze bum a cigarette?"

December 1, 2016

Yesterday's cigarette saga had perhaps the most appropriate ending imaginable:

I'm walking to the subway after work, having one final cig before going home, when this homeless guy comes up and asks me if I can spare a smoke. I tell him I'm sorry, but I've only got one left (this is true), so no, I can't spare one. He says that's alright, then asks if he can have the cigarette I'm currently smoking; he asks if I'll give him the cigarette literally right out of my mouth.

Now, this butt's been smoked down to the Camel logo—it barely has any tobacco left in it, maybe a drag or two. And it's been in my mouth for the past five minutes. But hey, if this guy wants to take my nearly finished cigarette and smoke it to the filter, who am I to stop him? I mean, I'm ten feet away from the subway stairs, about to toss the damn thing anyway.

I guess one man's spent smoke is another man's quick fix.

December 2, 2016

I'm outside my building right now, smoking a cig. This guy whistles at me—makes direct eye contact, whistles at me, and walks over. Says he's gotta get back to Coney Island and asks me for a dollar.

I tell him I don't much appreciate being whistled at; he gives me some utter nonsense along the lines of: "I wasn't whistling at you—I was just whistling in your direction. You got a dollar?"

I don't have any cash or change on me and go so far as to open up my wallet to prove it.

Then—surprise, surprise—he asks for a cigarette. I tell him I left my pack upstairs, which is the truth.

He asks me if I can give him anything, anything at all. I ask him if he likes candy, fish a mini Hershey's Krackel bar out of my pocket, and offer it to him.

"Oh man, I love that chocolate," he says, grabbing the candy right from my hand. He thanks me and turns away.

This gentleman immediately accosts the guy walking out of the bar below my apartment, saying he "need[s] some money to get out of dodge." Poor kid empties his pockets and gives this man all the change he has. It's not enough:

"C'mon, man, you don't got a dollar for me?" this guy asks. The kid walks back into the bar.

I'm still smoking my cig two minutes later when the same man approaches two young women and starts following them down the street, talking at them, catcalling. They're not having any of it and keep walking.

He comes back over to me, says I'm "good people" and moseys on down the street (but not before trying to sell me Klonopin; I politely refuse).

What a truly special guy. Like, I know it's within my ability to be mean to people and tell them to fuck off; I just seem to be having a problem with this, lately.

December 31, 2016

Six o'clock on the morning of New Years Eve, and I'm outside smoking a cigarette before I turn in for the night. This guy stumbles out of the bodega on the corner of my street and walks up to me:

"Yo man, lemme get a cig? I gotta walk back to Fort Greene. Can I just get a cigarette for the walk back?"

"Sorry, man—left my pack inside." (This is an obvious, bald-faced lie; I'd just bought a fresh pack of Camels from the corner store not two minutes beforehand, while this guy was in the store.)

"Aiight, well, can I just get the last couple pulls on yours when you're done?"

"Um, yeah, sure, okay."

"Cool, cool. Happy New Years! I'm'ma hang here till you finish up. But yo, check it: I'm listening to Fabolous. You know Fabolous?"

"Nah, no, not really."

"Ah, man. You know, like, he's my father? Fabolous is my father. Seriously, man. That's what I like to listen to when I walk home." He shows me the music playing on his phone, turning it up so I can hear the mellifluous sounds of Fabolous through his headphones.

"Uh huh. Really."

"Yeah, man! Check it out: this is what he got me for Christmas. This is what my father got me for Christmas." He shows me the two rings on his righthand middle and ring fingers; they're hideous, grossly enormous, covered with rhinestones or cubic zirconia or some such faux-bling.

"I gotta walk back to Fort Greene now."

"Mhm. Why don't you take the B54 bus?"

"I'm broke, man—just tryna get some money in my pockets before the ball drops tonight."

"Right. Sure. Well, here you go."

I give the guy the tail end of my cigarette and turn to go inside. This dude, clearly stinking drunk, walks away without so much as a "thank you." I can hear him screaming "Happy New Years!" at passersby as he saunters down the street.

Turns out Fabolous, who lives in Brooklyn, actually does have two kids. His oldest son is eight.

Happy New Years, indeed.

April 3, 2017

Immediately on exiting my apartment this morning, I was accosted by this guy standing in front of the corner store:

"Yo. Gimme a cigarette."

"Excuse me?"

"Lemme get a cigarette."

"Haven't you ever heard of the word 'please?'"

"Yo, fuck you, man."

It's going to be a good day.

April 6, 2017

Guy just comes up to me on the street with a cigarette in his mouth.

"Okay," I think, "he's not going to bum one from me but..."

"Yo man, can I get a light? Also, how do you work this thing? Somebody told me you could break this off."

It's a Camel Crush; he's about to break off the filter to turn the cigarette from regular to menthol. I show him how to crush the bead in the filter and light his cigarette for him. He thanks me profusely and walks away.

I hope cigarette karma exists, because this is going right in my "good deeds" tally.

June 5, 2017

One of the downsides to wearing super-tight jeans again is the lack of pocket space. My cigs—a nearly-full pack of Camel Filters—just fell out as I was running out of the subway and a Good Samaritan stopped to shout that the pack had fallen out of my hoodie pocket. Of course, this person didn't actually pick up my cigs and give them back to me. He just told me they'd fallen and then started yelling "I DON'T SMOKE CIGARETTES; I JUST SMOKE WEED. YEAH, WEED, MAN."

Like, alright, dude. On one hand, thanks for pointing out I'd dropped my smokes. On the other hand, goddamnit. Goddamnit all.

June 6, 2017

I'm standing outside my office smoking a cigarette, and there's an open water main on the street, leaving a disgusting smell wafting through the air nearby. I'm not particularly put off, but I see a woman walking past me start to dry heave—loudly and visibly, at that. And all I can think is "hah, what a wuss; she's definitely not from here," instead of "oh, that's a natural response to the smell of raw sewage permeating the air."

October 22, 2017

So, I'm outside a couple minutes ago, smoking a cigarette, as one does. And there's a random guy standing near my front door, hitting on this Puerto Rican woman who is clearly uninterested, so much so that she fakes a phone call and goes back inside the bar I live above. There's about five seconds of silence, and then this guy farts—loudly. "Excuse me," he says, before proceeding to ask me all manner of questions about my living situation: how long I've been in the neighborhood, how much I'm paying, whether utilities are included, whether I have a Hasidic landlord, and so on. I'm getting a little weirded out, so I kill my cigarette and pull out my keys.

Just as I'm about to go back upstairs, this other guy emerges from the bar and lights up a Marlboro Red. He offers me one—and, let's be real: That doesn't happen often—so who am I to refuse? So I'm now having a cigarette with the flatulent man, "Russ," and his buddy "Jimmy." Jimmy takes an interest when Russ tells him I live just upstairs, and he starts telling me about himself. He's twice-divorced, he tells me, and is looking for a new place.

Then, we start talking about the neighborhood. I tell him some of the usual stories about the craziness that sometimes ensues around here, what with all the frequent police and EMT activity because of the area's K2 problem and the fights that sometimes happen near our part of the street. Jimmy, it seems, has a lot of opinions about the people who live here—specifically, the people of color—and he has no problem casually referring to them using the n-word. "These n****rs," Jimmy says, "they don't wanna work; all they wanna do is rob, rape, and fight. You say you got a girlfriend, eh? Better walk her home from the train. You never know with these animals." Jimmy seems not to notice that he's talking to a brown kid who visibly winces every time he drops a racial slur.

I stub out my half-smoked Marlboro and thank Jimmy for it. Then, in one fluid motion, I unlock my front door, step inside, and make sure it's locked behind me before sprinting up the stairs. I think this is actually the first time a stranger's offered me a smoke in this neighborhood. Un-fucking-believable.

October 30, 2017

Just getting on the downtown A at Penn Station right now, in the middle of rush hour, I spy an open seat—well, not quite: The seat's got a bag in it. As I approach and fix my gaze on the seat, the man whose bag it is asks me, with notable sarcasm, if I want to sit down. He's not even saving the seat next to him; it's one of those L-shaped seating configurations and he's saving the spot across from where he's seated.

"Oh, you wanna sit here? Yeah, I can move my bag. I *was* saving the seat for a pregnant woman or an elderly person, but yeah, you can have it," he says loudly enough for the whole train car to hear. I'm not in the mood. I shrug, roll my eyes, and back off.

A woman gets on behind me, making it into the car a split-second before the doors close. The man goes out of his way to flag her down, move his bag, and offer her the seat, making a grandiose gesture of it. She's seen and heard my exchange with the man, and as she takes the seat, she gives me a sympathetic,

"Eh, whaddayagonnado?"-sort of look, and rolls her eyes in his direction.

The man goes on to explain to the woman that he was saving the seat for someone elderly or pregnant. She's now visibly offended and continues looking at me, more pleadingly now, clearly discomfited by this ridiculous display of pseudo-chivalry.

The train approaches Canal Street, and the man tells the woman seated directly next to him—not the one for whom he "saved" the seat, but a different stranger lucky enough to be a recipient of his kindness—that he's getting off at Fulton Street. Two stops away. Nobody asked, nor are there people blocking his egress.

As we come to the next stop, Chambers Street, he asks a portly man standing next to me if the portly man would like to take his seat when he gets off. At this point, the woman seated directly next to him, clearly annoyed, says (to the do-gooder, to the portly man, to me) that she's getting off at Chambers, so it really doesn't matter.

We stop at Chambers and the do-gooder starts to get up. He's halfway up when he pulls out his phone and straight-up fakes a phone call to his mother. He stands there, halfway out of his seat, blocking the whole bench. People are getting noticeably angry because there's an elderly, clearly frail man standing in front of the do-gooder. After about 30 seconds, he realizes this and offers the man a seat with a sweep of his arm, as if it were his idea to "save a seat" for this guy. The elderly man sits down; so does the do-gooder.

I can't take it anymore. I ask him if he's considered that he might be bothering the people around him, if he thinks it's right to do things like save a seat with a bag until a person he deems worthy comes along. He and I have a brief exchange, during which I tell him he's just *such* a paragon of subway courtesy and thank him mordantly for displaying his good works as an example for everyone else to follow. He says that it's a free country; that there was a time when the conductor would've made an announcement asking people to give up their seats for the elderly, infirm, or pregnant (that announcement is still made, by the way); and that these days, people make their own rules and don't adhere to courtesy. He says he's trying to get home, same as me. I tell him that's really weird that he should be incensed by people making their own rules, because that's exactly what he's doing right now; that yes, it's a free country, and I'm free to sit wherever the fuck I want on public transportation without having to worry about some jerk saving an open seat for whomever he rules deserving; and that I, too, am trying to make it home without being disturbed by people on my way there.

The do-gooder incredulously asks the people standing and seated nearby if he's disturbing them. A few nod.

As we pull slowly into Fulton Street station, the man finally, actually gets up and makes his way toward the doors. People are shaking their heads or just laughing at him outright. The portly man next to me asks if I want the open seat. He's sweating; I tell him it's all his.

He says: "Some people just have problems…" and the woman who got on behind me—the woman for whom the do-gooder was "saving his seat" at Penn Station—looks askance at the would-be Good Samaritan disembarking the train, agrees, and shrugs.

As the train doors open, we hear the man—now blocking other people getting off the train—ask someone if they'd like to sit down. There are no visible seats available. The people around me start laughing again. The do-gooder gets pushed out of the train before he can act or speak further.

Update (now, with 50% more anger!):

I get off the subway at my stop in BedStuy, and as I'm having a cigarette in front of my apartment, my buddy/neighbor/former roommate walks out of the bar below my place. We exchange pleasantries and he asks me about my day. He should know better, by now.

I begin recounting to him the events I've just experienced aboard the subway (see: my status post from about an hour ago). Right, smack in the middle of my story, a guy walks up to me, sticks his hand out, and demands a cigarette. He does not ask; he demands.

I tell him my pack is upstairs. He asks me for the one I'm smoking. It's just been lit, but he says I can just give the butt to him, no big deal. I say something like, "Man, I'm just trying to smoke this cigarette! Please!"

He gets pissed and mutters something vulgar under his breath as he storms off down the street. My friend tells me to chill, saying wisely that the man doesn't view me as a person, but as a cigarette dispenser. He makes an observation about it being funny how my story about being harassed on the subway mere minutes ago has just been interrupted by someone harassing me on the street.

As I finish telling my story, the man swings back toward us, a fresh cigarette in hand. I go to give him the tail end of my cigarette anyway. He mumbles something like "Yeah, have a good one," and saunters off.

UPDATE PART II:

Literally just now, as I'm standing outside, another cigarette in hand, finishing writing the words just above these, a woman walks up to me and asks me for money. She's qualifies her request by telling me I already know what she's going to say—I already know because over the past week, she's been camped out on my block, asking me the same shit every day.

No, I don't have any money, I say. Like I told her this morning, I just lost my job. She asks me to

go buy her a sandwich from the bodega, saying, "Now, I *know* you have a credit card... go buy me a sandwich; I'm hungry!" I don't have a credit card, and I tell her the bodega has a $10 debit minimum. This is the truth, but she argues with me, saying the minimum is $5 and trying to drive home her request for a sandwich.

I offer to run upstairs and grab her some apples—she says "apples ain't food!" She keeps pressing me for money. Finally, she asks for a cigarette. I relent, reaching into my pocket for my pack (of course I have my pack on me, but why would I admit that? I'd be out of cigarettes as soon as I bought it. Always, always say your pack is inside) and pulling out a cigarette for her, which she snatches from my hand before running after a group of businessmen who've just walked past us.

She sneers at me and, like the man who got the tail end of my cigarette ten minutes beforehand, mutters something vulgar under her breath as she chases the businessmen.

I literally just threw my hands in the air outside my apartment door and screamed "Jesus, fuck!" to no one in particular.

January 10, 2018

I can't be positive, because I have my nose in a book, but I am 99% sure a dude just walked through this subway car straight-up smoking a cigarette.

I'm not even mad—that degree of selfishness, that near-total disregard for the health and comfort of one's fellow man, it's, well, kind of amazing.

January 23, 2018

Last night, I'm standing outside my practice space in midtown with Jeremy; we're about to go in for our Sunday-night practice sesh. There's a gentleman waiting to get in alongside us, and he's having a smoke. A guy comes up to him and asks: "Hey man, could you spare a cigarette? I'll pay you a dollar."

The dude smoking the cigarette balks and starts mumbling about how he really can't spare a cig.

At this, I immediately pipe up: "Yo man, you can give *me* a dollar for a cigarette!" The cigarette and dollar are exchanged in short order.

And that, folks, is what you'd call a shrewd business move.

May 21, 2018

Some dude just walks up to me while I'm having a smoke and starts in: "Excuse me, man, can I have a—"

I glance up from my phone at him.

"...no?" he finishes before walking away.

I don't even need to say "no" anymore; I just stare.

May 29, 2018

Triggerettes: The brand for lungs as sensitive as you.

June 1, 2018

I'm outside at the moment, smoking what you'd call a "jazz cigarette," when a security guard from the small private security firm across the street approaches me.

"You—smoking!" he says in a tone that's either excited or accusatory—I can't quite discern which.

"Um, uh, yeah. Yes." I reply uncomfortably.

"...can I?" he asks, motioning to the spliff clutched between my sweaty fingers.

"Wait, what?"

"Smoke!"

I'm alarmed. Is this a trick? He's wearing his security guard uniform; I feel like he's poised to narc me out to his buddies. Stranger danger!

"I don't know you!" I exclaim, suddenly channeling Bobby Hill.

"Gah!" he yells before turning on his heels and loping off down the street.

Very sus. There's weird shit afoot.

August 15, 2018

Coming up the stairs at the West 4th Street station just now, I'm flagged down by one of the panhandlers who frequent the area. He says, "How about you, young man—spare some change?"

"Nah, but I can give you a cigarette. That okay?"

"Oh yeah," he says, "that'd be great."

As I'm getting a cigarette out of my pack, another panhandler comes up behind me and goes,

"Hey man, can I have your glasses?"

"Uh, what?" I manage.

He points at my yellow-and-orange $5 shades: "Yeah, can I have them? Please? I have a show to do tonight."

"Umm. No, man. These are my glasses…"

"C'mon, man! I got a show to do tonight!"

"Yeah, yeah, you and me both, guy," I say, walking away.

Even when I am willing to part with my precious cigarettes, it's not enough.

September 14, 2018

I think there's something wrong with me: I've bummed four complete strangers cigarettes today. No transaction, no exchange of a dollar per smoke, nothing. Just, "Yeah, sure, you can have a cigarette."

Help.

June 11, 2019

Things I will not judge you on:

- Anything you were born with or as
- Your job or socioeconomic station
- Whom you choose to fuck

Things I will absolutely judge you on:

- How many spaces you put after a period
- How efficiently you navigate public transportation
- Your cigarette-bumming etiquette

www.ingramcontent.com/pod-product-compliance
Lightning Source LLC
Chambersburg PA
CBHW070436010526
44118CB00014B/2075